How to...
LIVE FOR EVER

How to...

LIVE FOR EVER

By NICK ARNOLD

Illustrated by Tim Benton

OXFORD
UNIVERSITY PRESS

OXFORD
UNIVERSITY PRESS

Great Clarendon Street, Oxford OX2 6DP

Oxford University Press is a department of the University of Oxford.
It furthers the University's objective of excellence in research, scholarship,
and education by publishing worldwide in

Oxford New York

Auckland Bangkok Buenos Aires Cape Town Chennai
Dar es Salaam Delhi Hong Kong Istanbul Karachi Kolkata
Kuala Lumpur Madrid Melbourne Mexico City Mumbai Nairobi
São Paulo Shanghai Taipei Tokyo Toronto

Oxford is a registered trade mark of Oxford University Press
in the UK and in certain other countries

Series devised by Hazel Richardson
Text copyright © Nick Arnold 2001
Illustrations copyright © Oxford University Press 2001

The moral rights of the author and the artist have been asserted

Database right Oxford University Press (maker)

First published in 2001

British Library Cataloguing in Publication Data available

ISBN 0-19-910781-5

3 5 7 9 10 8 6 4 2

Printed in in Great Britain by
Cox & Wyman Ltd, Reading, Berkshire.

Contents

HOW TO LIVE FOR EVER

In Kyoto, Japan, there is a beautiful temple garden in which three fountains gush and splash. According to legend each fountain has magical powers. 'Drink from the first fountain and you'll become rich. Drink from the second fountain and you'll find love. Drink from the third fountain and you'll enjoy a long life.'

So which fountain would you choose?

Wouldn't most of us choose a long and happy life? For thousands of years people have dreamt of fountains of youth and elixirs of life – magical things that could make them live for ever. And the incredible thing is that this dream is about to come true! People are living longer than ever before and some scientists are talking excitedly about extending human life for hundreds of years! Find out how as you discover:

- killer diseases and how to beat them

- why your dog can expect to live longer than your hamster

- how to avoid stress and stay healthy

- the foods that can help you live longer

- how worms can teach us how to live for ever

- how to replace your old body bits with new ones.

I'd like a stomach, two kidneys and an eyeball please!

CHAPTER ONE

MEDICAL MARVELS

People who think they know about Science will tell you that all living things grow old and die. They claim that ageing and death are Laws of Nature. But there are some living things that seem to go on for ever.

In the heart of California's Mojave Desert is a dusty creosote bush. It's not much to look at, but this humble shrub, known as 'King Clone', is over 12,000 years old. Just think – it was alive before there were wheels or pyramids! It's even older than California's bristlecone pine trees – they are mere saplings at 5000 years old.

Young upstart!

If you take a peek through a microscope at a drop of pond water, you may be able to spot another amazing elderly organism – a tiny creature called a hydra. It multiplies by growing babies on its body like buds, but the adult hydra shows no sign of old age. And that's not all – certain roundworms cut in half will live as long as a worm that hatched from an egg. That means that if a roundworm were cut in half every few weeks it really could go on living for ever!

So here's the $64,000 question:

Well, humans are already living far longer than they used to. This is because of marvellous medical discoveries that help people survive diseases that would have finished them off in the past. Read on for a full medical report...

Medicine gets its act together ....

The practice of medicine started in China around 400 BC when the emperor ordered that only people with special medical training could be doctors. Meanwhile the ancient Greek, Hippocrates (460–370 BC) laid the foundations of medicine in Europe by training doctors to look for the signs of disease in order to spot what the illness was. This is called diagnosis.

It's chicken pox – I can spot that disease anywhere!

Mind you, the Greeks didn't get everything right. They thought that ill-health was caused by an imbalance of four vital fluids in the body – blood, phlegm, yellow and black bile. For 2000 years doctors believed this codswallop and cheerfully slapped squirming, slimy leeches on critically ill people. The patients were supposed to have too much blood and this grisly treatment was supposed to make them better. It never worked. Surprisingly though, leeches are still used in some types of surgery to keep the blood flowing!

For 2000 years, doctors treated sick people without understanding the actual causes of ill-health. And all this time, killer diseases such as the plague (a disease spread by rats and fleas sometimes known in history as the Black Death), and smallpox claimed thousands of victims. Then, in the 1790s, the first clues fell into place – all thanks to a cow, a milkmaid and a heroic little boy.

The first vaccination?

Country doctor Edward Jenner (1749–1823) was a real bore. He would rabbit on to fellow doctors about his belief that catching a skin ailment called cowpox would prevent the far more deadly disease, smallpox. But it was 20 years before he tested his idea – in a dramatic fashion. First he took pus from the hand of Sara Nelmes, a young milkmaid suffering from cowpox, and scratched it into the skin of James Phipps, the child of one of his patients.

➤

Can you imagine your doctor using you for medical experiments?

This won't hurt... MUCH!

Think that was bad? The next bit was worse, far, far worse.

James suffered the mild skin sores of cowpox: a few months later he was injected with pus from a smallpox sufferer. But hold on ... smallpox was deadly!

It was the worst disease in the world. If you want to know what it was like, imagine a face covered in sores that itched and rotted and scarred the flesh! And it killed one third of its victims. Would James suffer this terrible death? The anxious weeks passed, but despite a slight fever the boy remained healthy! Dr Jenner had proved his point and soon everyone wanted cowpox treatment. It was, in fact, an early form of vaccination.

What is vaccination?...........................

Every time you get ill, your immune system swings
into action to destroy the germs that are making
you sick. An army of tiny living units called white
blood cells identifies the attackers and makes
chemicals called antibodies that stick the germs
together. Then more white blood cells gobble them
up. Vaccination means giving the body weakened or
dead germs so that the white cells can get to know
them. Then they will recognize and fight the living
bugs if they ever get inside your body. Although no
one knew it at the time, the cowpox germ was similar
enough to the smallpox germ to fool the white blood
cells into thinking that they were the same.

I'd know you
anywhere!

At this point in time, doctors still didn't know about
germs or how they caused disease. This crucial
discovery was made by French scientist Louis Pasteur
(1822–1895).

Mr Bacteria – Louis Pasteur

Pasteur lived for his work. He worked so hard and was so keen on microscopes that he even used one to examine his food at mealtimes. In 1862 he showed that germs were tiny livings things (we now call them bacteria) that live in the air and cause disease.

Pasteur not only successfully grew bacteria, he also showed that injecting a chicken with a weakened supply of bacteria created an effective vaccine. Soon researchers were scouring the world for the bugs that caused disease and making vaccines to counter them. The development of the powerful electron microscope in the 1930s brought even more tiny germs (called viruses) to light. And so began a world-wide crusade against viruses and bacteria.

By 1980 humans had gained their greatest ever victory over disease. An international campaign wiped smallpox from the face of the Earth. Edward Jenner would have been dead chuffed – if he weren't already dead, that is.

The deadly cut ....

An understanding of germs wasn't just good news for the doctors – it made surgery far safer too. Let's take a quick time trip back to 1830.

This patient is having his injured leg cut off. The surgeon is rather proud of his unwashed apron encrusted with dried blood – it proves he's experienced.

But the patient is screaming because pain killing gases haven't been invented (they were first used in 1842). Oh well, at least the surgeon is quick – the best of them could whip off a leg in 30 seconds. Unfortunately, the patient's survival chances are only 50:50 – Yikes!

The problem here isn't pain or loss of blood. The problem is that the operating theatre is crawling with germs that happily make their home on the patient's wounds. The stump of the leg rots and the patient dies.

Germ-killer – Joseph Lister

Enter a rather unpunctual but very hard-working surgeon, Joseph Lister (1827–1912).

Inspired by Pasteur's work, Lister tried drenching his operating theatre in germ-killers. His favourite was carbolic acid, a substance used to disinfect sewers. In 1865 a young boy named James Greenlees was brought to Lister. The boy's leg had been crushed by a cart and there seemed only one thing to do – chop it off and hope that the boy lived. But Lister had other ideas.

He washed the boy's leg in that wonderful carbolic acid stuff and wrapped it in foil, allowing the broken bones to set. Normally the leg would have started to rot as bacteria got to work, but the acid killed the germs. In six weeks James was better! It was a medical marvel and Lister's fellow surgeons were slowly won round to the idea of using germ-killers. Over the years, banishing germs from the operating theatre has saved thousands of lives.

Meanwhile, outside the hospitals, life was unhealthy and short. Poor people often had to drink water that was full of sewage. Not surprisingly, diseases such as cholera, which are caused by drinking germ-laden water, flourished. In 1854 cholera killed hundreds of people in Soho, London. Fearless medical researcher John Snow (1813–1858) tracked the disease down to a particular water pump that stood a few metres from a leaking loo. People were drinking water swarming with cholera germs from the terrible toilet! Naturally, Snow was flushed with his success.

This was before Pasteur had made his discoveries about germs, so Snow didn't understand that cholera germs caused disease. But his work inspired doctors and politicians to campaign for clean water supplies and better housing. As living conditions improved, people became healthier and began to live longer.

And even more lives were to be saved and lengthened thanks to a lazy doctor who became famous because he went on holiday.

Fungus fun –
Alexander Fleming

In 1928 an untidy germ researcher left his London lab and set off on his summer holiday. Alexander Fleming (1881–1955) was too lazy to dispose of his dishes of growing germs, but he got a shock on his return. On one dish the germs had been attacked and killed by a mystery fungus. Actually Fleming didn't notice this, but someone pointed it out before the scientist washed up the dish. As a result of this discovery, millions of lives were to be saved.

At that time, Fleming realized that the fungus wasn't powerful enough to kill germs in humans, and nothing happened for a few years. Then in 1940 a policeman and keen amateur gardener Albert Alexander scratched himself on his roses. The scratch was deadly.

Germs from the thorns attacked his face and then his bones, and soon he was gravely ill. Would the copper come a cropper?

Science to the rescue?.........................

That's when scientists from Oxford University, led by a dynamic Australian named Howard Florey (1898–1968), started dosing him with a new drug – penicillin. It was made from the purified juice of a fungus similar to that discovered by Fleming. For a few weeks the treatment seemed to work and Albert recovered. But the juice began to run low, so they had to start recycling it from Albert's pee. In spite of their best efforts, the juice ran out and the policeman died. The lesson was clear – penicillin could save lives, but only if there was enough to go round.

Florey's colleague, Norman Heatley, helped an American firm to mass-produce the drug and by the end of World War II (1939–1945) penicillin was being used to treat injured soldiers. Millions of people were saved from disease and infected wounds. But more was to follow. Penicillin was the first of many new drugs called antibiotics, developed from natural germ-killing substances. In 1952, for example, Selman Waksman (1888–1973) made an antibiotic from a fungus that he found in the throat of a sickly chicken. And the new antibiotics proved their worth against killer diseases such as the plague.

Gotcha!

By the 1960s it looked like disease was going to be a thing of the past.

MEDICAL MIRACLES

Aren't we lucky to live at a time when medicine has put an end to disease? Now all we have to do is to work out how to live for ever!

Thanks to the benefits of modern medicine, better housing, cleaner water and more food, people are living longer than ever before. In the 1880s one in four children died before they were old enough to go to school. In any ten years of your life you would have had a one in ten chance of kicking the bucket. Most people didn't make it to 46 and fewer than one in four made it to 65. There was really nothing very good about the 'good old days'.

By the 1990s in the developed world most people were living to 76 and beyond. In 2000 one British family celebrated the arrival of a special baby.

21

For the first time ever in the world there were six generations alive at a single time. Besides the mum there was a granny, a great granny, a great great granny and a great great great granny! Isn't that GREAT news?!

You're looking great, great granny!

But people still die of disease. Not the plague or cholera, though these diseases are still lurking in poorer parts of the world where antibiotics are in short supply. No, people are suffering from other diseases, such as cancer and heart disease. And meanwhile some of the old favourites have been staging a comeback.

This chapter is about how doctors have been tackling these threats and how they have been dreaming up some amazing new technologies to help.

Cruel cancer

There's actually nothing new about cancer. Some Egyptian mummies suffered from the disease.

Egyptian daddies get sick too, you know!

But because cancer tends to develop later in life, in the past most people died before they could develop the illness. But now because people live longer, the disease is more common and it kills one in three people.

Cells in crisis

To understand cancer you've got to understand that the human body is made up of millions of tiny units called cells. Most cells are so small that even 50 placed in a line would stretch just 1 mm. It's possible that your body contains 100,000 billion cells. Don't even think about checking this — it would take you over 3 million years to count them all!

➤

10 million and 12, oh drat, I've missed one. I'll have to start again.

Most of the time the cells behave themselves. But sometimes they go a bit crazy. They start splitting quickly and in many parts of the body this can form a lump called a tumour. This is what we call cancer and it can damage the body if the tumour gets too big or if tumours start popping up in different places. Actually, cancer is not one disease, but 210 varieties — one for each type of living tissue in the body (such as skin, nerve or muscle).

Cancer treatment can involve removing the tumour by surgery, poisoning it by chemicals (chemotherapy) or zapping it with radioactive rays (radiotherapy). The problem with chemotherapy and radiotherapy is that they can kill off healthy cells too. But at last help is at hand. For decades scientists have been searching for a cure for cancer and now, hopefully, time is running out for these dreaded illnesses. New treatments are being developed and tested which doctors hope will be cancer killers in the future. So let's meet the magnificent four: gene therapy, gamma knife, polymer bullets and blood vessel inhibitors.

Gene therapy

Gene therapy means targeting deoxyribonucleic acid (DNA), the complex chemical that controls cell functions. (To find out about DNA and genes turn to page 47). Cancer is actually caused by faulty DNA in some cells that makes them divide all the time. Gene therapy tries to correct the fault by introducing the correct DNA to the affected cells.

Gamma knife

This treatment sounds like something from a sci-fi film, but it's actually quite straightforward. Instead of blasting the affected area with radiation, you target your firepower on the tumour. A gamma knife zaps a brain tumour with 201 beams of high-energy radiation from all directions. It's accurate enough to avoid damaging the healthy parts of the brain.

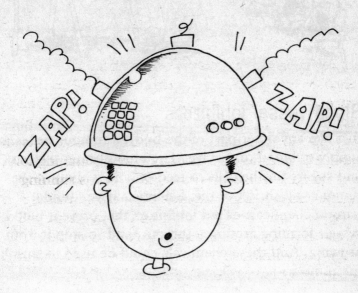

Polymer bullets ....

Instead of dosing the entire body with poisons, scientists are developing tiny capsules that deliver a steady dose of poison to the tumour. The capsules are made of a substance called polymer, designed to dissolve slowly inside the body releasing the poison over a set period.

Blood vessel inhibitors ....

Just like any other part of the body, a tumour needs a supply of blood to survive. The blood brings oxygen and sugars for the cells to feed on and without it the tumour will shrink or die. Scientists have found natural chemicals called inhibitors that prevent blood vessels forming around a tumour, and so stop it from growing. And these chemicals could be used to shrink the tumour.

Spies in the body ....

However, before doctors can attack a tumour, they
need to know exactly where it is. These days it's
getting easier to spot tumours wherever they're
lurking. Endoscopes are viewing tubes that can be
inserted into any opening in the body without doing
too much damage. There is also magnetic resonance
imaging (MRI), a technique that uses a combination
of powerful magnets and radio waves to produce a
computer-generated picture of what's going on in your
innards. It images the radio waves that bounce back
from each area to produce a moving picture of what's
going on in your body.

And this is
the best bit!

Horrible heart disease ....

In many parts of Europe and North America, heart disease is a bigger killer than cancer. The heart is a lovely bit of natural engineering. It's basically a pump that works non-stop for an entire lifetime, squirting blood around the body and to the lungs to receive oxygen from the air. It beats 4 billion times in an average lifetime, each beat powerful enough to send a red blood cell from your heart to the end of your leg and back again in just twelve seconds. But it can go wrong.

Broken hearts and battered brains.........

Fatty chemicals can build up in the blood vessels supplying the heart with blood. These can disrupt the heartbeat or place strain on the heart so that it wears out more quickly. The arteries that take blood to the major parts of the body can wear out and the build-up of damage causes blood clots. These stop the blood from flowing to the heart and may cause a heart attack, when the heart stops beating properly.

Blood clots or tearing of the brain's blood vessels can stop oxygen getting through, so parts of the brain die. The effects can be mild or severe. It's called a stroke.

Be an eternal life scientist:
TEST THE BLOOD SUPPLY TO YOUR BRAIN

WHAT YOU'LL NEED
- A watch or stopwatch with a second hand
- A pen and paper

WHAT TO DO
1 Take your pulse. Place your index finger lightly over the left side of your other wrist near the base of the thumb. This is your pulse — it is caused by the beating of your heart as it pumps blood through your body.
2 Count the number of pulses in a minute and write it down.
3 Go for a quick run. Take your pulse again and record the result.

WHAT HAPPENS?
Your pulse has dramatically speeded up as your heart works harder to supply your body with blood and oxygen.

Transplant technology ....

One way to deal with a failed heart or any other body bit is to replace it with a transplant. The first successful transplants were kidney transplants in 1954. Nowadays the list of body bits that can be transplanted is growing ever longer. Heart transplants and liver transplants are now pretty common. And transplants may have a big role in the future. In 1998 surgeons in Lyon, France gave a New Zealander an arm cut from a dead man. And in 2000 they sewed two new arms on to a Frenchman who had lost the use of his own arms in a firework accident.

Give us a hand, nurse!

But let's look further ahead – to the hospitals of the future.

Be ill at St Future's Hospital! All diseases catered for!

Relax on a robot bed that automatically measures your heart rate and blood pressure.

Trendy hospital pyjamas with intelligent sensors to monitor your blood sugars, heart beat and body temperature.

Bed supplies automatic emergency oxygen supply, heart massage and electric shocks to re-start your heart if it fails!

Need an op? No worries — let our specially programmed nano-robots (each the size of a body cell) do the job! You relax on your robot bed and let the tiny surgeons go to work inside your body!

Medical note – The robot bed and sensitive clothes could be made using the cheap silicon chip micro-sensors that scientists are predicting will be available within the next 30 years. Nano-machines already exist and tiny robot surgeons may be a reality in 40 years.

Did anyone mention diseases?...............

Just when you thought it was safe to sit on the bus next to someone who keeps blowing their nose, along comes a new army of diseases – and some old favourites.

New diseases that are appearing on the scene are viruses that have lived for thousands of years in wild creatures such as apes, mice, or blood-sucking insects. The diseases haven't done us any harm because we didn't have much to do with the animals that spread them. But thanks to our habit of destroying forests we are coming into contact with more and more new viruses, and as people travel more by air these diseases can spread quickly around the world.

Oh yummy. Some new meals are in town!

The worst so far is AIDS, a disease that kills by destroying part of the immune system. Without the immune system and its protection from germs, the body soon becomes very ill and may die. AIDS can only be contracted from infected blood or body fluids (and not from toilet seats or toothbrushes). Even so, 14 million people have already died from the disease.

To make matters worse some nasties from the past have come back to haunt us. The lung disease TB and the mosquito-spread disease malaria were thought to be under control. But then new strains of TB and malaria started to appear which couldn't be killed by drugs. The diseases were drug-resistant. Every year malaria infects 500 million victims, mainly in hot parts of the world, and TB is now one of the world's biggest killers.

Be an eternal life scientist:
DISCOVER DRUG RESISTANCE

WHAT YOU'LL NEED
- A large piece of brown paper
- A dark room
- 50 pieces of yellow paper (1 cm square)
- 50 pieces of green paper (1 cm square)
- Paper and pencil

WHAT TO DO
1. Scatter 25 pieces of yellow and 25 pieces of green paper on the large sheet of brown paper.
2. Pick out the first ten squares of paper that you see. Count how many are yellow and how many are green.

3   Bacteria increase their numbers by splitting in half. Switch
    the light on and add two bits of yellow paper for each
    yellow bit remaining and two bits of green paper for each
    green bit.
4   Repeat step 2 and 3 twice more.

WHAT HAPPENS?
1   There should be fewer and fewer yellow squares because
    these are easier to spot in the weak light. The yellow
    squares are like bacteria that are vulnerable to antibiotics.
2   There should be more and more green squares. These
    squares increase like antibiotic-resistant bacteria. The
    bacteria can multiply ever faster because there is less
    competition from other bacteria for food and for space.

But don't panic – doctors and scientists won't give up!
Modern medicine is fighting back with an armoury of
new weapons.

New improved drugs ....

Antibiotics stop bacteria dividing and some kill bacteria by destroying the protective walls that surround them. Drug-resistant kinds of bacteria pump antibiotic chemicals out of their bodies or make chemicals that switch off the antibiotic chemicals that try to attack them. Scientists are designing new antibiotics that disable the defences of the bacteria.

Vaccines ....

The best way to protect the body from viruses is using vaccines. In the 1960s measles affected 800,000 children a year, causing fever, skin rash and in some rare cases death. But thanks to a vaccine introduced in 1969, measles has all but vanished from Britain. In 1999 scientists developed a vaccine for Meningitis C, an infection of the tissue lining of the brain that killed over a hundred children every year in the UK alone.

And since 1993 scientists have been developing a new breed of vaccines based on the DNA of viruses. Just a harmless slice of this DNA is enough to prepare the immune systems to fight off the virus.

So despite everything we're still making progress. And medicine can still help us fight diseases that try to cut our lives short. But there's one condition we still can't cure – ageing itself. If you really want to live for ever then you'll have to do something to halt it. But what?

CHAPTER THREE

GETTING ON A BIT

Before you start reading this chapter, have a think about this. Do you really want to live for ever? Here's a legend from ancient Greece that might make you think twice.

A cautionary tale

In ancient Greece, the human, Tithonus, was going out with the goddess of the dawn, Eos. But the goddess noticed that her mortal boyfriend was growing older. Of course, being a goddess she never aged. So she asked her dad Zeus, the king of the gods, to make Tithonus live for ever.

Anything for you, bunnikins.

➤

So Tithonus didn't die — but he carried on ageing. His hair became white and his teeth fell out. He became slow and wrinkly and deaf and blind. Each day Tithonus would sing to himself in a voice that became squeaky and cracked with age. At last Eos could stand it no longer and she asked good old dad to get rid of him. Taking pity on his daughter, Zeus turned poor old Tithonus into a cicada insect! And, the story goes, Tithonus is still alive today. You might come across him singing to himself in his rasping little voice and looking as ancient and dried-up as ever.

Got the message? It's no use living for ever if you can't avoid the effects of ageing. But what exactly are these effects? And what causes them? The next pages will show you what to look out for.

BEFORE   AFTER

WARNING!

Before inspecting your grandparents for signs of ageing you ought to know that few older people suffer from all of these effects and they might be quite upset if you tell them they do!

1   Wrinkles. Old people have plenty of these. As you get older, the skin loses cells and becomes less springy and elastic. As the skin fails to spring back into shape after folding, it gradually creases into wrinkles. (To make one wrinkle try frowning 200,000 times.)

2   Sagging skin. As the skin becomes less elastic it droops down under the influence of gravity. This is especially obvious under the eyes and chin (causing a double chin) and the ear lobes.

3   A man's hair thins on top but often sprouts from the nostrils and ear lobes – yuck! Scientists aren't too sure why this happens. Hair turns grey because each hair loses colour and becomes hollow inside, reflecting the light in a way that makes the hair appear grey or white.

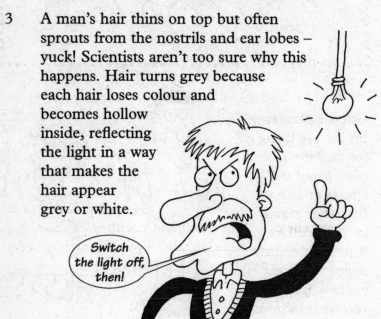

Switch the light off, then!

4   The heart, lungs and muscles weaken. This is partly due to cells dying off and partly due to lack of exercise.

5   Older people often suffer from stiff, swollen joints. This painful condition is called arthritis.

6   The eyeballs and their lenses bulge slightly making it hard for the eye to focus on close-up things. Older people often need glasses to correct their vision.

7   An old person's sense of smell and taste weakens as cells die off in the smell receptors of the nose and the tastebuds on the tongue. By the age of 70 a person has lost 50% of their sense of smell.

8   An old person's hearing may weaken as the bones inside their ear becomes stiff. Cells die off in the hearing mechanism of the inner ear.

9   Cells may die off in a region of the brain that
    controls the storage of memory. Although the
    memory remains as good as ever, an older
    person finds it harder to recall the information.

At least
I can remember
when my memory
was better!

Be an eternal life scientist:
DISCOVER WHAT HAPPENS TO OLD SKIN

WHAT YOU'LL NEED
- Sticky tape
- Scissors
- Two identical balloons
- Two marbles
- A ruler
- Paper and pen

WHAT TO DO
1   Sticky tape a marble at the end of each balloon (that's
    opposite the end you blow through). Measure the length
    of both balloons.
2   Blow one balloon up and then release the air ten times.
3   Measure its length again.   ➤

Hormone hopes.....................................

So that's what's happening. Now for the tricky bit – explaining why. You see, ageing doesn't have a single cause, it has several! They include:

☞   changes in hormone levels

☞   wear and tear

☞   ageing cells

OK, so what are hormones? Hormones are chemicals that float around in the blood and produce changes in the body. For example, hormones made by the thyroid gland in the neck control how fast the body's cells burn up sugar to make energy. And human growth hormone made by the pituitary gland in the brain makes the body grow.

As a person grows older the amount of growth hormone in their body reduces. But what happens if the body is given extra hormones? In 1990 Daniel Rudman at the Medical College of Wisconsin, USA, gave Fred, a retired car worker, injections of human growth hormone. The results were incredible. Fred began to look younger and his muscles got bigger.

Unfortunately, he also developed aches and pains and when the injections ceased his muscles shrank again.

The dangers of everyday life..................

Now for the second cause of ageing. Don't panic –
but every day your body is under attack! Day after day
the pressures of life are ageing your body. To find out
more we're going to take a quick look at leaves.

Be an eternal life scientist:
DISCOVER HOW LEAVES GET DAMAGED

This experiment works best in late summer or early autumn
when the leaves have been growing through the summer
months.

WHAT YOU'LL NEED

✒ A selection of damaged leaves from different plants

✒ A hand lens

WHAT TO DO
Study the leaves and use the hand lens to examine the leaves
more closely.

WHAT HAPPENS?
You may find several kinds of damage: holes made by various
munching insects, slugs and snails; there may be brown areas
or spots caused by disease or by the plant dumping waste
chemicals in the leaf. In other words, plants suffer from wear
and tear over time.

I need a holiday!

But what's this got to do with humans?

Humans also suffer from wear and tear (although luckily our bodies can repair themselves, which is why our wounds heal). Here are a few of the rigours of everyday life our bodies face:

- harmful chemicals such as bleach can damage and dry the skin

- tobacco smoke is bad news for the body. It wrinkles the skin, clogs the lungs with tar and triggers lung diseases and cancer. Chemicals in the smoke enter the bloodstream and cause changes that can clog blood vessels and make heart disease more likely.

- teeth decay and fall out because of the kinds of food we eat and because we don't always clean our teeth properly

- heavy drinking of alcohol can damage the liver and make it harder for the body to process food or break down poisons

- wounds and some skin diseases can leave scars

- joints can be overused and develop arthritis (see page 41)

- ulcers can cause scarring on the inside of the stomach and guts

- looking at the sun too long can damage eyes

- sunlight contains ultraviolet rays that can damage the DNA in skin and make it look all dried-up. Sun damage to DNA can also cause skin cancer.

But quite apart from wear and tear, your cells are dying off and this also causes ageing. To know more you really need to know a bit more about DNA.

DNA and its secrets

Scientists had long suspected that cells contained a chemical code that controlled how they developed. Then, in 1953, Francis Crick and James Watson worked out the structure of this chemical, DNA. DNA is like a ladder that has been twisted into a corkscrew shape by a circus strongman. The rungs of the ladder are a combination of just four chemicals called base pairs. And the code to make the cell grow and develop is the exact order of the base pairs in the ladder. Inside the cell each unit of DNA is organized into a structure called a chromosome of which humans have 46 (23 pairs). Got all that?

Every feature of your body, for example your eye colour, is coded for by units of DNA known as genes and made up of thousands of base pairs. Human DNA contains over 100,000 genes but in recent years scientists have been mapping where each gene is located on the chromosomes. You may have heard of this vast undertaking – it's known as the Human Genome Project.

Yes, this is a vast job. If you lined up the entire DNA in just one human cell it would be almost 2 metres long. If you wrote the human DNA code down, it would fill a 500,000-page book and if you attempted to translate the code into English you would fill over 1000 huge encyclopaedias!

Where's the bit about blue eyes?

Smashed up cells ....

Much of what we call 'ageing' is caused by cells in each part of the body gradually dying off. But why do cells die? Why don't they last for ever so we can too?

A cell might be tiny but it's incredibly complicated. Imagine a cell as a tiny factory. Like every factory it uses power. Ripping apart tiny molecules of glucose supplied in the blood produces the power. This creates energy, but it also creates harmful electrically charged chemicals called free radicals that can damage DNA.

Although DNA has its own repair mechanisms, damage can build up and eventually prevent the DNA from controlling the cell. Sometimes the cell starts dividing and causes cancer. And worse still, any repair work that is possible seems to slow down as a person grows older!

49

Cures for old age ....

As you can imagine, people will try anything to reverse the signs of ageing. Below are just a few of the crazy things people have tried in the past. (*Don't* try any of these at home!)

Blood baths

In the 1600s Hungarian Countess Elizabeth B'athory bathed in blood to stay young. She even tried drinking it, too. This mad woman even had a handy machine designed for stabbing and bleeding young girls. Unfortunately for Liz, bathing in blood doesn't keep you young, and is against the law. The crazy Countess was locked up for life after murdering over 600 girls.

Doggy snacks

How about eating ground-up bits of dog or guinea pig? In 1889 Professor Charles Brown-Sequard tried it. He thought it would make him feel a new person and help him live loads longer. Surprise, surprise. The potty prof pureed his pets for nothing! The body's immune system destroyed the injected material. Brown-Sequard ended up covered in sores from the injections and died at the not especially old age of 77.

Yoghurt for youth

Nobel Prize-winning scientist Elie Mechnikov (1845–1916) ate live yoghurt (that's yoghurt containing living bacteria). He believed that the living yoghurt bacteria would stop any harmful bacteria moving in. Although yoghurt is a genuinely healthy food, sadly there's no proof that it actually extends life.

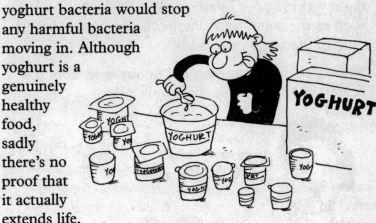

So, is that it? Perhaps you are wondering if you've got any chance at all of living for ever, when ageing affects us all and the remedies aren't up to much. Well, wonder no more. There are things you can do to slow down the ageing process. Read on and find out!

CHAPTER FOUR

FIT FOR LIFE?

This chapter is about how to live longer. So let's meet a person who ought to know the secret if anyone does – the oldest woman in the world!

Pampo's story

One January day in 1875 a baby girl was born on the West Indian island of Dominica. She was christened Elizabeth, but she became known to everyone as Pampo. When she was a little girl, Pampo had no toys and she never went to school or saw a doctor. Her mum was too poor to afford any of these luxuries. As soon as she could walk, Pampo worked from dawn to dusk in the sugar cane fields.

Sometimes her mum sent her to buy food from the nearest shop – a whole day's walk away.

You'll have to go back. You've forgotten the butter!

Pampo never had any great adventures and the most exciting event of her life was her wedding day when she visited a local town. Sadly, she didn't have a happy life – her only son died in his forties and she lost contact with her remaining family. But Pampo lived on.

At the dawn of the new millennium, Pampo was still living in her shack by the sea just as she had in the previous century – and the century before that. She had never gone away on holiday, never had an electric light, never owned a phone or a car. She was 125 years old and yet somehow time had passed her by. What was her secret?

Pampo's secret ....

Pampo told a reporter that the reason she lived such a long time was her healthy diet. She ate lots of fresh fruit and vegetables and drank fresh coconut milk.

Although Pampo didn't know it, these foods are rich in chemicals called anti-oxidants. Cells that protect DNA from free radical damage use these. (Remember? Free radicals are the electrically charged chemicals that can damage DNA.)

Be an eternal life scientist:
MAKE A LIFE-EXTENDING FRUIT SALAD

WHAT YOU'LL NEED
- Some fresh dates (if you can't get these, the dried variety will do)
- A coconut
- A banana
- A mango

WHAT YOU DO
1. Ask an adult to drill a hole in the coconut and drain out the milk.
2. Chop up the banana and ask an adult to chop the mango and the dates, removing the stones.
3. Ask an adult to saw the coconut in half and scoop out some of the flesh from the coconut.

This is taking years off my life!

4. Pour a little coconut milk over the fruit and eat chilled.

And now for some more healthy tips for a long life.

Live long, live healthy

1　Clean your teeth twice a day. That means brushing lightly with circular movements and using a soft nylon brush.
2　Take plenty of exercise. This doesn't mean running a marathon every day. It does mean cycling or walking daily and not being too lazy to run errands.

Time for both your walkies!

3　Avoid eating too many sweets, chocolates and crisps, especially just before a meal when they may spoil your appetite.
4　Never stay out in the sun for more than a few minutes without using a strong sun-block cream. Wear long sleeves and long trousers if you are in the sun for long periods.

But maybe there's another factor that affects how long you live. And you really can't do much about this next one.

Do women live longer than men? ....

Not necessarily! Figures show that on average women die at an older age than men do, but that doesn't mean they live longer! The figures show that the important factor is that men die younger! And here's why.

Young men spend more time outside the home and are more likely to die in accidents or by violence. As they grow older, men are more likely to get certain cancers (it's thought that a hormone called oestrogen that women's bodies make helps to protect them from these). However, if men don't smoke or drink alcohol and eat healthy food, they can still live as long as women. And talking about food, here's a rather odd question for you to ponder.

Is lack of food good for you? ....

In the 1930s scientists made an amazing discovery. Mice kept from birth on almost one third their normal intake of food, lived one third longer than normal.

I'd do anything for for a lump of cheese!

Their diet included the vitamins they needed to stay healthy, and oddly enough they had as much energy as before. This finding has been repeated with other creatures, such as rats, worms and apes. So could it be true for humans? Could a human live to be 150 just by missing din-dins? And what's causing this effect?

Scientists think that lack of food switches DNA off. When this happens, the DNA is tightly wrapped in a layer of protective chemicals. This acts like bubble wrap shielding the DNA from damage by those nasty free radicals.

He's got a very delicate temperament.

HANDLE WITH CARE

Well whatever the cause, some scientists are already cutting down on their food intake in a bid to live longer.

WARNING!
Don't cut down on your food when you're growing up.
Your growing body needs all the grub it can get!

Healthy body and healthy mind ....

If you're really serious about living for ever, you'll need to look after your mind as well as your body. It's no use staying healthy and youthful if your brain turns to jelly! So it helps to learn new things whenever possible (why not read some more books in this series?) and practice your problem-solving skills with puzzles or computer games and enjoy lots of hobbies. And you'll also need to learn how to deal with the horrible monster called stress.

Sickening stress

Stress is how you feel when you're all keyed up — pulse racing, muscles tense, palms sweating. Stress was once quite a useful bodily reaction. Just imagine — it's the Stone Age and you've got to fight a cave bear.

▶

Well, a little stress might come in handy here. The fast pulse is a sign of oxygen-rich blood zooming around your body to those tensed, action-ready muscles. The sweat flowing is helping to keep those heat-producing muscles from over-heating your body.

So, stress is great for preparing your body for action. But when you feel stressed because you've got to do something like a test, it just makes you feel bad. And too much stress can even make you ill! Sickening — eh?

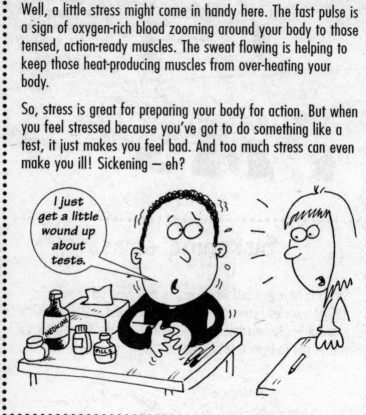

Study after study has shown that stress causes ill-health. In the 1970s scientist Hans Sleye found that stressed lab animals were more likely to fall sick. In 1991 an experiment using humans seemed to confirm this. A group of American university students were exposed to colds – some of the students were feeling stressed and some weren't. Nearly half the stressed students caught colds, but only a little over a quarter of the relaxed students ended up with red noses.

This finding is not to be sneezed at – it seems that stress switches off the immune system leaving the body more vulnerable to germs.

So if you want to stay healthy it helps to relax and enjoy life. So pour yourself a long cool drink, put your feet up and read this next bit. It's time for another glimpse into the future – this time it's a visit to Dr Well's Health Clinic.

Time for a check-up?

Visit Dr Well's Health Clinic in person, or visit it in virtual reality on the Internet!
Get your personal DNA CD checked out for free radical damage!
Find out your personal diet, mental well-being and exercise requirements.
Check your personal stress index. Keep stress at bay!

This isn't as far-fetched as it may sound. Doctors are beginning to realize that being relaxed and happy is an important part of keeping patients healthy.

TIPPETTY
TAP

TIPPETY
TAP

The DNA CD check should be possible once human DNA has been completely decoded and understood in about 20 years.

What's that? You don't like healthy food and exercise, and cutting down on food sounds too much of a hardship? OK, there's an another way to live longer – if parts of your body are failing you, why not simply buy some new bits? Yes, it really is possible!

CHAPTER FIVE

TIME FOR A NEW BODY?

So you fancy a new body?

ENJOY A MONSTER BODY!

BARON FRANKENSTEIN'S MONSTER BODIES ARE MADE FROM SEWN-TOGETHER BITS OF CORPSES. HE'LL PLOP YOUR BRAIN INTO THE MONSTER'S SKULL SO THAT YOU CAN CONTROL ITS BODY!

Don't panic! We won't really be trying that particular treatment. There are actually three options for getting a new body and living longer.

1 Rely on transplants as and when they are needed to replace your worn-out body bits.

2 Get some artificial body bits made and use them to replace the faulty living bits.

3 Grow replacement body bits from your own cells.

Transplant troubles..............................

There are two problems with transplants. First, the body's immune system attacks any tissue that it doesn't recognize – this is called rejection. (Baron

We don't want this new heart!

Frankenstein's monster would soon have died if it ever really existed, because each bit of the body would reject the other parts.) That's why transplant patients need powerful drugs that switch off their immune systems for a while to stop this from happening.

Second, there is a shortage of spare organs that can be transplanted from dead people. (We're not talking musical instruments here by the way – an organ is a body part with a particular job.) Scientists are trying to get round the shortage by breeding pigs with human DNA. When the pig organs are transplanted into humans, the fact they contain human DNA should give them more chance of being accepted by the recipient's immune system.

Bionic body bits ....

The other option is artificial body bits. In 1998 a Scottish hotelkeeper was given a bionic arm.

It was controlled by nerve signals from the remains of his old arm and fitted with a complex series of pulleys and gears. The arm could twist and grip and bend. It was even covered in a layer of silicon that looked like real skin. And as time goes by, scientists are inventing more and more artificial body bits.

Body bits

Here's a selection of artificial body bits. Some are still at the experimental stage but should be widely available in the next few years.

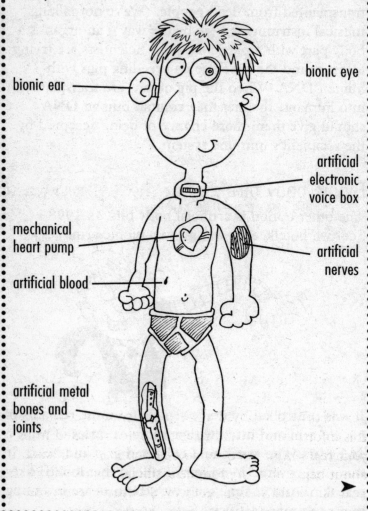

bionic ear

bionic eye

artificial electronic voice box

mechanical heart pump

artificial nerves

artificial blood

artificial metal bones and joints

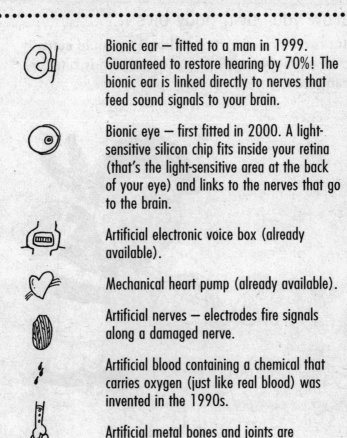

Bionic ear — fitted to a man in 1999. Guaranteed to restore hearing by 70%! The bionic ear is linked directly to nerves that feed sound signals to your brain.

Bionic eye — first fitted in 2000. A light-sensitive silicon chip fits inside your retina (that's the light-sensitive area at the back of your eye) and links to the nerves that go to the brain.

Artificial electronic voice box (already available).

Mechanical heart pump (already available).

Artificial nerves — electrodes fire signals along a damaged nerve.

Artificial blood containing a chemical that carries oxygen (just like real blood) was invented in the 1990s.

Artificial metal bones and joints are available now.

One of the hardest bits to make artificially is a brain. After all, your brain stores your memories and personality. If you had an artificial computer brain all this information would have to be downloaded from your real brain. Even so, some scientists are talking about being able to produce artificial brains within the next 50 years! So you really could live for ever – as long as you don't mind being a bionic robot!

Grow your own body bits ....

But there's another possibility. You could actually grow your own cells to make spare body bits for transplant.

Because they contain your very own DNA code, your immune system will think the new organs are part of you and won't attack them. Sounds interesting? OK, here's how to do it.

First, you're going to need to know about stem cells. These are the cells that you'll be growing your organs from. The amazing thing about stem cells is that they don't age and die like other cells – remember?

Stem cell secrets.................................

You have got stem cells in the lining of your mouth and guts and in the marrow of your bones. Their job is to divide constantly and make new cells.
Without them your mouth and guts would be worn away by your food and spit. (Yuck!)

Your stem cells are almost as old as you are. Every human being starts off as an egg fertilized by a sperm.

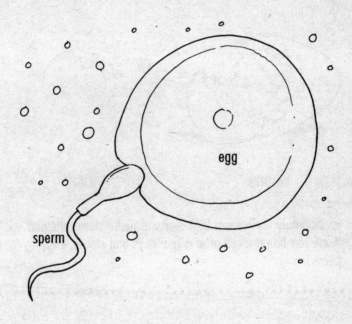

The egg and sperm each contain half the DNA needed to code for building an entire human baby. The sperm's DNA fuses with the egg's, and the egg begins to divide. In a few days it becomes a ball of cells and each cell has the ability to divide and form new organs. These are your stem cells.

Make your own body bits

Take some of your DNA from a cell in your skin and stick it in an empty egg — a hen's egg will do. By the way when we say 'empty hen's egg', we don't mean an empty hen's eggshell — we mean the tiny cell inside the shell that could have developed into a chick. This cell is empty because its DNA has been removed.

WRONG   RIGHT

Immediately the human DNA starts to make stem cells and these can be removed after a few days and stored. Easy-peasy!

The fact that stem cells carry on dividing for a very long time could prove very useful. One day it might be possible to inject stem cells directly into any area of the body that needs regenerating. The stem cells would be programmed to work in just that area and you wouldn't need messy, painful transplant surgery!

But for the moment this isn't possible. And unfortunately, scientists aren't too sure how the stem cells know what body part to form. In 1998 scientists at the University of Wisconsin, USA grew cells for different body parts from stem cells simply by changing the food that the cells were being fed on. But DNA and chemical signals amongst the stem cells may also be important.

And we'll give this one some lung food!

LUNGS

HEART BRAINS

Scientists think that by providing a scaffolding of polymer for the cells to grow, they can encourage the cells to form a new hand or a new heart, blood vessels or skin or whatever you fancy. And they have already managed to grow a human ear inside the skin of a living mouse.

I keep hearing things!

Amazing alternatives...........................

There is an amazing alternative to growing your own stem cells. Cancer cells also divide without ageing, and one type of cancer has the ability to form body tissues such as teeth and hair in the wrong parts of the body. Scientists are planning to use these cancer cells to re-grow worn out body parts. And that's not all.

Scientists at the University of Philadelphia, USA, have found that when mice have their immune system switched off, they can regenerate their own bodies. Mice with damaged ears and tails can grow new ears and tails. They can even replace some of their nerves and bone and muscles. Although the scientists are not really sure why this happens, it's not unique. Salamanders and newts also re-grow parts of their bodies, and certain lizards can lose their tails and re-grow them.

If you could do this you wouldn't age. Whenever a body bit wore out, you could simply grow a new one. The only problem is that without an immune system, germs would attack you. The only way to survive would be to live in a germ-proof bubble.

Oh, so you don't fancy spending eternity in a plastic prison? Well, there is a substance that keeps your cells alive for ever, and guess what? It's inside your body at this very minute! Find out more in the next chapter.

CHAPTER SIX

MEAN GENES

Ageing affects different people in different ways. Some people look ancient at 40, while others look young and glamorous in their 70s. This is why guessing someone's age can get you into trouble!

You're not bad for 70.

What a cheek – I'm only 43!

Looking youthful and living to a good age seems to run in families. So there must be something that people are born with that keeps them alive longer and looking young. There is – and that something is DNA! After all, you inherited half your 46 chromosomes from your mum and half from your dad.

How does DNA affect ageing? ....

Every length of DNA has its own fuse that turns the DNA into a ticking time bomb. The fuse is called a telomere, a protective cap that fits over the ends of each chromosome.

Be an eternal life scientist:
FIND OUT HOW
A TELOMERE WORKS

WHAT YOU'LL NEED
- A length of string
- A piece of sticky tape
- A washing-up brush

WHAT TO DO
1. Wrap a piece of sticky tape around one end of the string.
2. Brush the other end of the string roughly with the washing-up brush and then hit that end of the string on the end of a table ten times. Now brush and hit the uncovered end of the string again.
3. Repeat step 2 with the end of the string that is protected by sticky tape.

WHAT HAPPENS?
The unprotected end of the string becomes worn and frayed, but the protected end of the string should remain undamaged. The sticky tape works like a telomere protecting the end of a chromosome.

I'm afrayed I've had enough!

Unfortunately, each time a cell divides the DNA replicates too and some of the protective telomere is worn away. The longer the telomere, the longer the cell can survive. When the telomere is all gone, the DNA is unprotected and can easily be damaged.

Cells that live for ever ....

So how come stem cells don't wear out? Well, it's because of a substance called telomerase. Telomerase rebuilds the telomeres. Stem cells (and cancer cells) make telomerase and rebuild their telomeres. That's why they don't age like ordinary cells. And the making of telomerase is controlled, (surprise, surprise) by the DNA. So you know what that means, don't you? In your own body you have the power to make cells that live for ever!

So a cell that makes this amazing stuff need never die! Scientists have even found the gene that orders a cell to make the substance and added it to the cells of an old man. The cells started dividing and even after 400 divisions they were still going strong. The old chap's cells had gained eternal youth!

But don't jump for joy just yet! Yes, if your body had this treatment it would last for ever, but there are a few nitty-gritty problems to overcome first. Namely, how do you get the telomerase gene to every cell in your body? And how do you switch on and off the gene at will so that the cells don't divide all the time?

Meanwhile, scientists are searching for other genes in our DNA that might have an effect on ageing and how long we live. Their inspiration for these experiments comes from other animals.

Ancient animals ....

Some animals live for a very long time. Flounders, lobsters and sharks grow bigger as they get older but they show no signs of ageing. The only reason they ever die is because of disease or injury. Tortoises not only move slowly, they age slowly too. The oldest giant tortoises lived over 175 years.

The oldest large animal is the elephant. Elephants live for up to 80 years. The oldest birds are parrots and eagles. They both live over 40 years.

77

Be an eternal life scientist:
WORK OUT THE AGES OF YOUR PETS

WHAT YOU'LL NEED
✌ An old cat or dog. (A friend, someone at school or a neighbour might have one if you don't.)

WHAT YOU DO
Note down the age of the animal and then work out its equivalent in human years. A cat year is the equivalent of five human years. A dog year is the equivalent of six or seven human years.

Now answer the following questions.

1   Does the animal walk awkwardly or is it stiff-legged?
    Yes. This might be a sign of arthritis.

2   Is the animal thin or over-weight?
    Yes. Elderly cats tend to eat less and look thinner as their muscles waste away. Elderly dogs usually eat as much as ever and put on weight because they exercise less.

3   Does the animal show signs of hearing loss?

Yes. Older cats and dogs show signs of deafness. Also the animal might not react to sounds as quickly as a youngster might.   ➤

4 Does the animal pee in the house?
Yes. Ageing shrinks the kidneys and makes the bladder less able to hold urine. Ageing might also affect the animal's memory so that it forgets the training it received when it was young.

WHAT HAPPENS?
In some ways cats and dogs age like humans. They lose their hearing and develop problems that humans suffer in old age, such as heart disease and arthritis. But cats and dogs age faster than we do. Few cats live more than 20 years, and most dogs die between 8 and 15 years old.

So why does my dog live longer than my hamster?

Scientists aren't sure, but there's a theory that answers this question and explains the whole reason why animals age. It's all to do with natural selection.

Select for survival

Over millions of years every species (type) of plant and animal changes form — a process called evolution. For example, 60 million years ago the first horses were just 30 cm tall! Evolution is powered by something called natural selection. Here's how natural selection might have worked with penguins.

At one time all penguins were black. Seals swimming under-water could easily spot their dark tummies and would dart up to catch and eat them. Some penguins had white tummies and the seals couldn't see them so easily. The penguins with white tummies had genes that made their tummies white. More of them survived to pass the genes on to their young and over time all penguins were born with white tummies.

What do penguins wear on their heads?

Ice-caps!

And now here's the crucial bit. An animal can have really terrible ageing genes and still pass the natural selection test! Even if an animal grows old quickly and dies young, as long as it lives long enough to produce offspring it will pass on its genes. This explains why your dog ought to live longer than your hamster.

Hamsters can produce young when they are just ten weeks old. And once a hamster has had a few babies, there is no reason why its ageing genes shouldn't kick in. So within 16 months most hamsters have gone to that great big hamster wheel in the sky.

But a dog can be a year old before it gives birth and it might take another three months before the puppies can leave their mum. So dogs need to live longer to be sure of passing on their genes. It takes years for humans to have families and to bring up their children, which is why we live far longer than either our dogs or our hamsters!

Learning from animals...........................

Scientists have found that we share surprisingly large amounts of our genes with our fellow animals. We share a gobsmacking 40% of our genes with a roundworm and 75% with a mouse.

Humans are like mice? Impossible!

Already scientists have found genes in a type of worm that help extend its life. They have also found that one of these genes seems to be similar to a human gene that keeps cells alive.

So here's the big picture. Your genes and DNA are pretty vital. And if they're not up to scratch, the best that science can offer is the chance to get the right genes, or maybe a squirt of telomerase to protect your DNA. But if you're really keen to live for ever and don't mind being cold, there is yet another possibility to consider. Fancy the deep freeze?

CHAPTER SEVEN

COLD COMFORT

Just one look at the ancient bag of peas in your freezer should convince you that very cold temperatures preserve things. But can the cold really help humans to live longer?

Animals as different as bears and bumblebees go into a state of suspended animation in cold weather, known as hibernation. In this state their bodies slow down, their heartbeat eases up and their cells use up food far more slowly.

DO NOT DISTURB UNTIL SPRING

Could hibernation help animals to slow the effects of ageing? We don't hibernate, of course. But there have been cases of people who have fallen into freezing water and survived without air for up to ten minutes because the cold has so slowed the rate at which their cells needed oxygen.

A real cool character

It's true that a frozen human can last a very long time. One cold night, over 5000 years ago, a traveller went to sleep in a little hollow high in the Alps, the mountains that separate Austria and Italy. He never woke up. In 1991 walkers found his frozen body preserved in ice and surrounded by his clothes and tools and weapons. Ötzi, as the body became known, had achieved a kind of immortality.

Some people believe that it might be possible to freeze their dead bodies and then thaw them out at a later date and restore them to life. To do this, the bodies are drained of blood and filled with glycerol anti-freeze. Next they are submerged in liquid nitrogen at a bitterly cold temperature (-196° C). This technique is known as cryogenic suspension.

But before you start filling in the application forms you should know – things can go wrong.

Cold comfort? ....

The biggest problem with cryogenics is that no one knows how to bring a frozen body back to life. And while being preserved in liquid nitrogen any water left in the body would have turned to ice, splintering and destroying the cells. The dead frozen bodies would be too damaged to bring back to life, anyway.

However, there may be hope for the future. In the 1990s scientists found out how to preserve organs for transplants. The organs were soaked in a liquid containing sugar and dried with a chemical called perfluorocarbon and stored at low temperatures.

And some Antarctic fish can survive temperatures of below freezing because their bodies contain natural anti-freeze chemicals. So will we one day be able to preserve an entire human body? And could that person be revived?

Well, if you don't fancy ending up as a human ice-cream, there are other ways to extend your life. Now here's your chance to put them into practice!

CHAPTER EIGHT

IMMORTALITY AT LAST!

So you've read this book and reckon that eternal life is just the ticket! Well, unless you're getting on a bit you don't have to worry about ageing just yet. So why not wait 20 years and volunteer for the first ever life-extension programme?

Step one 2020 – Go for a check up

All volunteers for the programme begin by seeing their doctor for a full check up. Your doctor will make a CD of your DNA and check it for any sign of disease or damage.

Step two 2020 – Still at the doctors

Hopefully your DNA is fine but it might need a course of telomerase treatment to lengthen your telomeres. (They're the protective caps on your chromosomes. Remember?) If the worst comes to the worst, you might need gene implants in some of your organs to ensure that the telomerase gene is switched on for a few years.

Step three 2030 – The robot hospital and organ bank

It is time for a routine operation to remove some of your stem cells and freeze them for the future. (The cells can be frozen so fast that they don't suffer ice damage.) After the nano-robots have done their job, you sign autographs and take part in a 3D holographic TV chat show. (Yes, joining the life-extension programme has made you a real celebrity!)

So how does it feel to live for ever?

Step four 2030 – At home

Back home it's time for a virtual reality chat with Wanda, your personal health adviser. She's been programmed by your doctor to tell you what exercise and diet you need to keep your body in tip-top condition. You'll need to take a complete range of vitamins and anti-oxidants, but luckily Wanda is not suggesting the dreaded reduced food diet! By the way, Wanda is a computer-generated being so she won't age. And she can even teach you computer games to keep your brain in good condition!

Step five 2060 – Back at the doctor's

Life has been great so far and you're still feeling young and fit. But the doctor suggests that your muscles could do with boosting. Luckily human growth hormone injections are now possible without fear of side-effects. You decide to enter for the World Senior Citizen Olympics.

Step six 2070 – Back at the robot hospital

You only popped in for a routine check-up and they offered you the chance to have a complete gene makeover! All your ageing genes are switched off and the genes that keep you young are replaced.

Step six 2080 – Back at the hospital

Despite all the treatment, your kidneys and heart are not what they used to be. And your vision and hearing are weakening. Now it's time to use those stem cells that you stored away 50 years ago. In a few months the hospital grows you a new heart and kidneys and these are transplanted into your body. You opt for the latest bionic eyeballs and ears and leave hospital with better vision and hearing than you ever had before!

Step seven 2120 – Back at the hospital

You're over 100 years old, but thanks to regular hormone treatment and telomerase top-ups you look and feel about 30. Unfortunately, your lungs and guts are showing signs of ageing and you're wheezing and suffering from indigestion. But technology has once again come to your rescue. Injections of stem cells can now regenerate your organs without transplants. Phew!

Step eight 2130 – Back at the hospital

There's a problem – your old brain is showing signs of ageing. The brain contains your personality so you can't simply slot in someone else's. And because brain cells don't divide you can't boost them with fast dividing stem cells. So you opt for the latest artificial bionic brain computer.

All your memories are downloaded into the machine and it's placed inside your skull. Once the computer is switched on it's easy to forget that your brain is a machine. Oh well, it should be good for a few hundred years! You celebrate by telling a historian about life back in the 2000s.

Step nine 2160 – Back at the robot hospital

Deep down you feel uneasy. Maybe you've done it all?
You've reached level 600 on every interactive virtual
reality computer game on the Internet, you've
travelled to every country in the world twice and
you're bored of your great, great, great, great, great
grand-children. Fortunately Wanda has the solution –
a short cryo-rest. So you arrange to be deep-frozen for
a short time, say about 50 years.

Step 10 2210 – That's better!

You wake up feeling much refreshed, if a little chilly.
Technology has moved on and now there's loads more
things to do. Scuba diving on Mars is a must now
they've put an ocean there and ski-ing on Pluto
sounds really cool. Yes, you're really looking forward
to the next 200 years! Life is good and you just can't
get enough of it!

CHAPTER NINE

WHO WANTS TO LIVE FOR EVER?

Eternal life sounds brilliant doesn't it? But is immortality everything it's cracked up to be? On the one hand you can have an eternity to do all the things you enjoy. But on the other hand, you've got all the time in the world to get bored of eating your favourite food, to get tired of the same old films and music. Even to get bored of your best friends and their endlessly repeated jokes.

You told me that joke 150 years ago!

And what about all those old people? You're not going to be the only person living for ever. Once they realize how well it's worked, everyone will want the same treatment. And the government will have to make sure that everyone has a chance to benefit from this technology even if they can't afford it. It would be unfair if the only people who got to live for ever were rich, greedy old millionaires. And once there are lots of older people around, how will they be treated?

It is fact, not fantasy, that in the future old people are going to be fitter and healthier and there are going to be rather a lot of them. Even without everlasting life treatment, by 2050 in China alone, there will be 270 million people aged over 65. And all these people must be housed and fed and cared for. Perhaps people will stop having children to stop the world getting over-crowded.

Ultimately, no matter how long life is, it's what you make of it that really counts. Surely 70 good years are better than 700 boring ones? So get out there and make the most of however many years you have got to live on this planet. And remember – Never say die!